# RAISING WELL-BEHAVED, BALANCED DOGS

## THE DOG PARENT'S GUIDE SERIES

SUNNY LUTHRA

All thanks to Mr Cesar Millan, his teachings inspired me
to become a dog behaviourist and help people understand
dog psychology.

# Contents


*Preface*      *vii*

1. Introduction      1

2. Understanding Dog Psychology      3

3. Rituals Of Dogs      8

4. Understanding Behavioural Issues      14

5. Calm Confident Companion Skills      26

6. Next Step - Join Help Centre      34

Conclusion      35

# Preface

The quality of every relationship depends on the quality of communication. The quality of communication depends on the quality of understanding. To have a meaningful deep relationship with dogs, we must understand them first.

# CHAPTER I

# Introduction

Are you raising a dog?

Do you think about how to understand your dog and have a strong relationship with him/her, or how to improve or change your dog's behaviour?

Are you trying to find innovative ways of communicating with dogs to replace old, outdated ones?

If you've answered "yes" to any of these questions, welcome to our group!

Hi, I am Sunny Luthra. As the author of this book, I have years of experience working with and caring for dogs. Plus, I have conducted 100s of socializing sessions and given consultations to many dog parents on different behavioural issues. I know what it takes to create a well-balanced dog, and I'm excited to share my knowledge with you!

This book is for dog parents who want to raise a well-balanced dog. It covers topics such as understanding dog psychology and the rituals of dogs that will help your dogs to live a calm confident happy life. This book is also for dog trainers or dog behaviourists who want to understand more about how to raise a well-behaved balanced dog.

This book is not for dog parents who are looking for a quick fix to their dog's behavioural problems. It is also not for people who are not willing to put in the time and effort to understand their dog. If you are not prepared to commit to this, then this book is not for you.

This book is different from most dog training books out there. This book is not about teaching you tricks or commands to get your dog to do. This book is about understanding your dog's psychology and using that knowledge to raise a well-balanced dog.

This book is divided into four chapters, each dealing with a different aspect of raising a well-balanced dog.

The first section looks at the psychology of dogs and how to use this knowledge to better understand your dog.

The second section looks at the rituals of dogs and how to perform them appropriately.

The third section looks at common behavioural issues and their solutions.

The fourth section mentions 5 skills that you can help your dog learn to enjoy life with you.

The fifth section is about your support system.

I hope you enjoy reading it as much as I enjoyed writing it.

# CHAPTER II

# Understanding Dog Psychology

Dogs are not like humans. They have different needs, desires, and motivations. This means that we need to understand their psychology in order to raise them properly. If we try to use methods based on human psychology, both the dog and the human parents will often be frustrated.

It is important to understand that dogs are not humans and to treat them accordingly. This does not mean that we should not love or care for our dogs, but rather that we need to respect their difference and work within their limitations. By understanding dog psychology, we can provide our dogs with the best possible life and avoid many behaviour problems.

Each animal species has its own psychology. Tigers have a different psychology than zebras. Dogs have their own psychology too. They live differently and have their own rituals. The biggest mistake people make is assuming that dogs have the same psychology as humans do. This is the main reason why dogs sometimes have behavioural issues.

One major difference between humans and dogs is that humans dwell in the past, we think about the past, often carry the burdens from the past and get depressed or we worry about the future, get anxious and overwhelmed but dogs always live in the moment, in the present.

Many a time I get approached by people who tell me that their dog is aggressive, he bit another dog. When I look at the case I don't focus on why the dog bit another dog - I look at which of the needs of the dog are unmet due to which he's developing behavioural issues.

If we fulfil the needs of the dog it's unlikely that he would develop any behavioural issues.

We have to understand that dogs live in the present. If we change our own attitude and behaviour today, we will start noticing the change in our dogs instantaneously.

A dog is an animal first, then species and then a breed. We give them names such as buddy, Bruno, Leo, and Shine, but they don't have any names in their natural habitat.

So how can they identify each other in the wild?

They recognize one another by smell and energy.

Animals communicate through energy and every animal naturally respects a calm and assertive source of energy. Animals identify each other through energy. Otherwise, how would they know who's a predator and who's the prey?

Dogs only like to follow a calm and assertive energy source. So if we want to have a deep connection with our dog we have to learn to project calm and assertive energy.

Dogs like to work for their food and shelter. Most dogs instinctively like to work for their food, team up with other dogs and hunt for their food and create a safe space to live. But if you don't give a dog an opportunity to work, it will make the dog unstable. For instance, taking the dog out for a walk is extremely important for a dog. The walk is not just a means for them to relieve themselves. A structured walk - something we will learn about in detail in the next chapter - give the dog a chance to work. We need to understand this and bring about a change in our mindset and stop taking a walk of the dog casually.

Dogs feel good when they have a job to do. They feel like they are worth something and this makes them humble. We need to give them a job so they can feel fulfilled.

If you pay close attention you will find that in the jungle a crocodile waits patiently to hunt and as soon as a zebra comes close he attacks. A puppy waits for its mother to come and feed him. Waiting for food is a natural phenomenon. We need to teach our dogs what waiting with patience means. When we go to feed our dogs, dogs should not be excited. We should make them wait, sit down calmly, before feeding them. This is how we mimic their natural habitat. Waiting comes naturally to them.

We even cause phobias in our dogs unknowingly. For instance, I once got a case of a dog who used to be very scared by the sounds of vehicles. We found out where did it all begin, we found out that once the dog was hit by a vehicle and at the time the human accompanying the dog got very upset, frustrated, picked up the dog, started shouting at the driver, and this escalated the whole situation and converted into a phobia for the dog. If at that point the dog which got hit was accompanied by a dog instead of a human, the scene would be very different. The dog would not have panicked. He would've projected calm energy that would make the hurt dog feel calm, secure and confident.

We mustn't forget that it's a dog that we're dealing with and not a human. If a dog gets a trauma or phobia, we are not supposed to get stressed about it. We have to project the energy of calmness and confidence just like any other dog would have.

We nurture a lot of unwanted behaviours in dogs. For instance, if we see a dog scared or under stress, our first reaction is to give them affection. But a human can understand why you're giving affection in such a situation because they can rationalize. Humans can understand that you're giving affection so that they can come out of it and feel happy. But a dog cannot rationalize. Whenever you give affection to a dog you are going to nurture the state of mind the dog is in. So if a dog is under stress and you're giving him affection, you're nurturing the state of nervousness in the dog. If a dog is barking at you and you're giving him affection, you're nurturing the state of excitement in the dog. Your affection is in fact a very powerful tool and every time you give affection, you will nurture the state that the dog is in while being given the affection.

When a dog is born only the nose is open. Fifteen days after birth his eyes get open and it's only after 21 days that the ears begin to function. So his nose is very powerful. But every time we meet a dog we create a lot of sounds "Hi baby! Hello Baby!". We are not supposed to do that. When we call out to a dog we don't give him a chance to use his nose. He has to use his ears and that's what he uses to relate to you. But how does a dog relate to his mother? Through his nose. He respects his mother through the nose. The more a dog uses the nose, the calmer he would be and more balanced. The more he uses his eyes and ears, the more alert he would be. And a constant state of alertness leads to unwanted behaviours.

So every time you meet your dog, project calm and assertive energy. If you desire a deep connection with your dog, meet him with calmness. We have to become the source of calm and assertive energy.

For example, when we look at Mahindra Singh Dhoni, he's calm and assertive. He's focused on whatever he wants and pursues it seamlessly. So whenever you meet a dog, pay respect to his nose, eyes and ears. Let him come and sniff at you. Don't create a sound. The more he uses a nose to connect with you, the deeper your bond will be. The dog will then look at you with respect as you are the harbinger of calmness and security in his life. This would certainly deepen your bond with your dog deeply. So every time you meet a dog, project calmness and assertiveness.

Living with discipline, rules and boundaries come naturally to dogs. It's a part of their habitat. Lack of discipline leads to instability. You will have to consciously work out a set of rules and boundaries for your dogs at home, then only our dog will respect us.

As soon as a pup is born the mother starts applying rules and limitations on their baby. If we don't put these rules, boundaries and limitations on the dog, the dog will put these rules and limitations on us.

Many people claim that all German Shepherds behave a particular way, all Rottweilers are like this, all labradors act like this, all indies are like this - NOT TRUE. Breeds denote a skill set in a dog. It's like a cloth you wear from the outside. All dogs are the same from the inside. All dogs have some common needs and in addition to those, they have needs of their particular breed.

So if we look at a Husky, they live to travel long distances. They can travel for days at a stretch. Other dogs can also travel but Huskies have the capacity to travel much more. Indies have territorial behaviour which is present in all dogs in some fraction but it's more evident in indies. Most indies protect their territory and hunt for food but when you bring them inside four walls of a house, you are not fulfilling their innate needs and this can create a lot of issues in them. It's not the breed but how well you understand dog psychology.

So don't forget dogs are an animal, species and breeds and we need to fulfil the needs of all three.

# CHAPTER III

# Rituals of dogs

Dogs are social animals and in the wild, they live in packs. In order to have a balanced dog, you need to provide him with the same structure that he would find in the wild.

Here are the 5 rituals to create structure in your dog's life:

1. Walk Ritual
2. Discipline Ritual
3. Socializing Ritual
4. Feeding Ritual
5. Play Ritual

## *Walk Ritual*

The Walk Ritual is probably one of the most important ones because it's where your dog gets to explore and release energy. A good 30-60 minute structured walk two times a day is necessary for your dog's physical and mental health.

By structured walk I mean when the dog is walking beside you or behind you.

So, how should we walk our dogs?

1. You take the dogs on walks at a fixed time.
2. You take the dogs 2+ walks/day and the walk should be 45+ minutes long.
3. You initiate the walk calmly without making any big fuss about it.

4. The dog is calm when you pick up the leash.
5. The dog is leashed and he is sitting beside you when you open the door.
6. You lead the walk by going out of the house first.
7. During the walk, the dog is walking beside you or behind you.
8. You understand that walk is for both of you, it's for the leader-follower bond between you and your dog.
9. You are leading the walk by walking briskly and giving a break of 5 min to the dog after walking 15-20 mins.
10. You do not use a mobile phone or lose focus and stay present with the dog.
11. You follow the same structure of leading the dog while entering into the lift, going out of society or coming back.
12. You are consistent

Please write your schedule for walking your dog, mention the time and who's responsible for giving him two mandatory long walks every day.

(Ex: I am responsible for taking my dog on long structure walks. I am going to take him on a walk at 7 AM and 5:30 PM, I am going to make time. I am going to make sure that I and my dog both follow the structure of a perfect walk. I understand a structured walk is very essential if I want my dog to live a balanced life)

## Discipline Ritual

During the Discipline Ritual, you are teaching your dog right from wrong. This is an important part of their education and must be done with patience and consistency. Shouting or releasing frustration is not the dog's way, they discipline each other by remaining calm and assertive.

In the wild, dogs who break the rules of the pack are disciplined by the dominant balanced dogs. This is important because it keeps the pack safe and ensures that everyone knows their place within it.

As the leader of your dog's pack, it is your job to provide this discipline when necessary by remaining calm, confident and consistent.

Rules, Boundaries & Limitations are part of mother nature, you must be clear about them and ready to create for your dog.

Examples of rules, boundaries and limitations:

1. No entry in the kitchen.
2. No jumping on furniture(Sofa, bed, etc.) without permission.
3. Not allowed to chew or take any object other than you provided to them.
4. Not allowed to steal any food from the dustbin or table.
5. You do not get angry or frustrated if your dog breaks any rule.
6. You choose a calm assertive way to help your dog understand even if you have to discipline your dog 100 times, you do it with calmness and assertiveness.

Write what rules you are going to create for your dog and then sign them so that you will not get frustrated but will work on yourself if you get frustrated or angry at your dog.

## *Socializing Ritual*

The Socializing Ritual is essential for dogs because it helps them develop social skills that they will need throughout their life. It's also a great way for them to meet new people and animals.

This is not about you socializing your dog with other humans or dogs but it is about the way you meet with your dog on a daily basis.

The way we meet with dogs and the way dogs meet with each other is totally different. We use a lot of sound and excitement while meeting our dogs but in their natural habitat dogs meet with each other calmly and use their nose.

Proper Socializing Method:

1. Practice no touch, no talk, no eye contact so that the dog can use his nose while meeting you.
2. Give affection only when your dog is calm.
3. Do not give affection when your dog is jumping on you.
4. Whenever you give affection to your dog, you are going to nurture the state of mind he is in.
5. Excitement and happiness are two different emotions.
6. Excitement is unstable energy in animals.
7. Practice calmness and project calm-assertive energy while meeting your dog.

Write that you are going to meet your dog by practising no touch no talk no eye contact and honour his identity of being a dog. Whole family members should be on the same page.

## *Feeding Ritual*

The Feeding Ritual is another important one because it establishes rules and structure around mealtimes. By providing regular meal times and following a set routine, you are teaching your dog that there is predictability in his life which he needs for comfort.

Food is a big reward for your dog, so giving it without awareness of its importance can make your dog or break your dog.

Feeding Ritual Guidelines:

1. There should be a fixed time for the meal.
2. Meals should always be after 20-30 minutes of a long walk, dogs love to earn their meal, it keeps them humble towards food.
3. You should be calm and should not start the feeding ritual by creating excitement.
4. The dog should wait calmly for the food.
5. Be there when your dog is eating his meal.
6. Pick up the bowl if your dog shows no interest in eating his meal within five minutes and provide the meal at the scheduled time only.

Write who is responsible for feeding the dog and be clear that you need to project calmness and follow the proper feeding ritual guidelines.

## Play Ritual

Last but not least, the Play Ritual is essential for dogs because it helps them release energy and have some fun! Playing with your dog can be as simple as throwing a ball or playing tug of war with obedience.

Dogs have a playing circuit in their mind, just like us. They must play every day but playing every time is damaging for their behaviour, they are using play as a way to release their energy which means they are using excitement which is unstable energy in animals as a way to release their energy, you need up the duration of their walk.

Play with obedience:

1. Decide a time for play with your dog.
2. Be consistent.
3. While playing bring your dog to a certain level of excitement and then practice obedience with them. (ask him to calm down or sit)
4. You will learn to control his impulses and he will learn to listen to you even if he is excited.
5. Practice daily, it creates wonder, your dog will become more obedient with every repetition.

Write who is responsible for playing with him and at what time you will play with him.

By following the five rituals of dogs, as outlined in this chapter, you can create a balanced dog who is happy and content.

# CHAPTER IV

# Understanding Behavioural Issues

I grew up with many dogs(15+) but none of them had issues that I faced in dogs when I started my dog behaviourist journey in 2016.

I knew that dog parents innocently are doing mistakes in raising their dogs because no dog is born aggressive, you will not find any aggressive puppy but they start developing behavioural issues once they start getting influenced by us humans, just because we lack understanding of the species "Dogs".

Most dogs live a balanced life(calm, submissive, peaceful) when they are with a balanced pack.

When a dog becomes unstable in the pack then all members of the pack start correcting him and if they can't then they remove him from the pack, for us this can be harsh but this is the law of nature, the survival of the fittest.

When we bring a dog into our life, we start raising him using our own psychology but as I mentioned in previous chapters dogs have different psychology and different needs.

When we fail to fulfil their needs then they start developing behavioural issues, that's why understanding dog behaviour is very important if we want to raise well-behaved balanced dogs.

In this chapter, I am going to cover the most common issues I had a chance to work on.

1.  Aggression
2.  Hyperactivity

3. Separation Anxiety
4. Obsession / Fixation
5. Phobia
6. Low Self-Esteem

## Aggression

Aggression is one of the most misunderstood behaviours in dogs because it is not an issue in the first place.

Most dog behaviourists or dog trainers or dog parents make a mistake by treating aggression as an issue but actually, aggression is a symptom of an underlying issue.

Now, suppose if a person is suffering from malaria(Issue) and he is having a headache(symptom), do you think treating a headache is the right approach or should we treat malaria?

I don't have to answer that, but I think I cleared my point that we need to work on the root cause of the aggression.

The big question is what is the root cause?

Well, aggression in dogs is not natural and it is important to understand because most people think that aggression is natural or this breed is aggressive or this is my dog's personality to be aggressive, we have to clear these false beliefs so that we can work on the real issues.

During my journey, I came across two types of aggression:

- Dominance Aggression
- Fearful Aggression

## *Dominance Aggression*

When you observe dogs in their natural habitat, you will find some dogs do project dominance over other dogs but they are not aggressive.

See, dogs are born with one of two traits, either they are followers or they are leaders.

99% of dogs are born followers and only 1% are capable of leading, that's how mother nature keeps the balance, otherwise, there will be clashes.

When you bring a dog into your life and because of your lack of knowledge of dog psychology, you unintentionally fail to provide leadership which makes your dog take the leader position, because dogs are pack animals and a pack cannot function without a leader.

Most dogs are born followers and if you give the responsibility of leading to a follower dog, then the dog becomes 'insecure' 'anxious', or 'frustrated' which creates aggression when dominance comes into the equation.

So if we provide leadership to the dog then there is no need for the dog to take it.

Most people think that they can take the leadership by being dominant on the dog and the meaning of dominant person they have in their mind is someone who is strict, angry, and of yelling nature.

A strict, Angry, and yelling nature person is not a leader but a dictator. Both are different personalities.

We humans must understand and learn how to become leaders of dogs.

"Before we move forward, first we have to understand that leadership is necessary for all the dogs and not just the dogs who are having behavioural issues, if you provide leadership then most dogs will not develop any behavioural issues at all."

## *Fearful Aggression*

This issue is very unfortunate because prevention is very easy but the cure is a long journey.

If the dog gets afraid or fearful often and humans don't know how to behave in that situation then eventually any fearful dog can become aggressive.

In all cases of fearful aggression, one thing was common in the ways humans were behaving with their dogs.

The most common mistake they were making was the timing of the affection, every human was giving affection to the dog when the dog was under stress.

The intention of humans was to give comfort but that's not how a dog's mind works.

Whenever you give affection to the dog, you nurture the state of mind the dog is in.

By giving affection when the dog was nervous, humans were nurturing nervousness in the dog, and that's why it is important to understand dogs otherwise we will keep on making such mistakes which later can manifest as serious behavioural issues.

I remember a very interesting case I handled in the initial days of my dog behaviourist journey, at that time OhMyDog Parenting Model(a Video course for raising well behaved balanced dogs) was just in my mind.

So I was handling a case of a nervous dog who according to her owner was very unpredictable (animals are very predictable, it's just our lack of knowledge of dog behaviour we don't know what they are up to.) and has attacked and bitten her on multiple occasions.

To learn more about her behaviour I took her in and started observing her and found out her aggression is just because of her fear or when she becomes uncomfortable.

The way her human was giving affection to her was very intense for her and that's why most of the bite happened when she was receiving affection.

I kept her with me for 15 days and in 15 days no biting accident happened, she spent most of her days in peace.

I just followed the rituals of dogs which I mentioned in the previous chapter. She became calm and confident in just a matter of a couple of days, which was amazing for me and her human to witness.

Her human started following all the steps and changed her own behaviour first to help her dog become more calm, confident, and loving.

## *Hyperactive*

"My Dog jumps on my guests"
    "My Dog is always hyper or excited"
    "I am afraid my dog's jumping can hurt kids"
    "I want my dog to meet calmly with everyone"
    "I don't know why my dog is always hyper"
    "He is always in a mood to play"
I hear concerns like these almost every day and people think that issue is in the dog but in reality, humans don't know how to channel the energy of the dog.

In every breed, you will find dogs with 4 types of energy.

1.  Low
2.  Medium
3.  High

## 4. Hyper

The meaning of level of energy is the amount of mental stimulant a dog requires to feel fulfilled, if he doesn't feel fulfilled then it will be very difficult for the dog to calm down.

Recently a family called me for their hyper dog who used to jump on everyone, pull on the walk and kept on barking whenever the family was discussing something which was making any type of communication happen among family members very difficult and unpleasant.

When I reached their home and met with the dog I found out that the reason behind the excitement of the dog is the behaviour of the humans with the dog.

Everyone in the family and in their building used to meet with a lot of excitement with the dog, so the dog learned only this way(excitement) of living life.

As soon as I started behaving calmly with the dog, the dog became calm, it felt like he was waiting for me the whole time to come and teach their humans the right way of raising a dog.

The most common mistake humans make while meeting their dog or any dog is they project a lot of excitement because they think excitement is happiness but excitement and happiness both are different emotions.

This family was also doing the same, whenever they come back home, they open the gate, take the name of the dog with a lot of excitement, so the dog comes running and starts to jump and humans give affection to the dog.

On a daily basis, the dog is learning excitement means affection, jumping means love, so he keeps on doing the same for his humans.

But, real happiness for a dog is when he is calm and submissive. Not when he is excited. In mother nature excitement is unstable energy, you will not see any zebra jumping in a forest.

I asked them to start nurturing calmness and ignoring excitement.

I also told them to meet the dog calmly.

Within 2-3 days the dog stopped pulling them, stopped jumping, and stopped barking.

They were facing this issue for 2 years but if they knew how a dog's mind works then they and their dog wouldn't have to go through so much frustration.

## *Separation Anxiety*

Separation Anxiety is not natural in dogs because in their natural habitat they never get separated from the pack.

Pack represents the power to a dog and getting separated from the pack means death to them.

In humans, it is pretty natural for us to get separated for work and other things so we must help dogs to understand that it is ok to get separated from the pack.

Now how to do that?

See, in dogs, they have a resting state which we need to trigger if we want to leave them behind four walls alone.

You can trigger the resting state by giving a long structured walk twice a day.

When you leave your dog behind four walls without being exercised properly which can help him naturally go under a resting state of mind, they feel excited.

When the energy of excitement in dogs doesn't get any outlet because they are behind 4 walls, they feel trapped.

In old times when dogs used to feel trapped, they usually dug their way out which is not possible in today's concrete households and that is why you will see scratch marks on doors and windows.

The excitement in the animal world is unstable energy when it gets blocked, it becomes anxiety which the dog releases by pacing, barking, or destroying the house.

Give proper exercise to your dog before leaving him for long hours.

Nurture Calmness more than often.

Don't create the energy of uncertainty by feeling bad about leaving your dogs.

You will not see any anxiety in dogs in their natural habitat, but they start developing issues once they start getting influenced by us humans.

Let me tell you about one case of severe anxiety in a dog which we successfully corrected, by corrected I mean we helped the dog be calm when left alone.

He was very destructive and used to howl, scratch windows and doors, torn sofas and every mattress apart just to reach his human.

His human was consistently getting complaints from society about the nuisance her dog was creating.

She contacted me and we started working on him immediately..

The first thing we did was asked the human to follow the rituals of dogs for 7 days and after that, we started helping the dog to understand that alone means good, alone means calmness.

How did we do that?

Rituals of dogs can help any dog become more calm and confident, and we needed that. So after Implementing the Rituals of dogs, we started the second stage of the training.

Now, understand this, the more the dog is insecure, the higher will be the level of separation anxiety.

What we need to do is to create a safe environment for him at home but you will say that my home is already safe for him, yeah you know this but your dog doesn't believe the same.

For him separation from the pack means death, it means he is not capable of handling the situations on his own, so we are going to change this.

As I mentioned before, following the rituals of dogs is a must for every dog parent.

Now, let's begin the second phase.

Our Motive is to change insecurity which is the cause of separation anxiety into calmness and confidence.

You can do these by following these simple steps:

**Create A Place For Your Dog**

By this I mean your dog should have his own place, his own bed, maybe a corner in the house, or a crate, there should be something which we can use to create an association of calmness.

So make a permanent place for your dog, it is going to help him immensely in becoming calmer.

**Start Leashing Your Dog**

For some people leashing the dog means cruel, but trust me that is not right. The dog is insecure, that is why he or she is getting anxious, making your dog habitual of being leashed inside the house.

Start leashing your dog when you are at home so that you can correct it by saying NO calmly with confidence (don't get frustrated) whenever the dog becomes unstable.

Increase the duration of leash time, dog must remain on leash 1-2hrs daily in his place.

**Start Training His Mind That The Pack(You) Will Be Back:**

So your dog is leashed at his place, without saying anything or giving eye contact, go out of the house, shut the door, and come back immediately.

Do this 4-5 times every day, and start increasing the duration every day, every dog is different so you have to experiment with your dog and keep on practising this step.

This will create an association in the dog's mind that the pack goes out and comes back as well.

This is exactly the same strategy that we used to help many dogs suffering from separation anxiety.

Please be consistent.

## *Obsession / Fixation*

Obsession in dogs is a state in which the dog is excessively interested or focused on something. This could be an object, person, or activity. Dogs become fixated on things for a number of reasons, such as fear, anxiety, boredom, or curiosity. When a dog becomes fixated on something, it can be very difficult to get him to focus on anything else.

Dogs that are fixated on a particular object or activity may become agitated if they are unable to engage in that activity or get close to the object. They may bark, whine, pace back and forth, or try to escape. In some cases, dogs may become aggressive if they feel threatened or frustrated.

If your dog is fixated on something, it is important to find a way to redirect his attention. You may also need to increase the amount of exercise and mental stimulation he receives.

## *Phobia*

Dogs can develop phobias just like people can. A phobia is an irrational fear or anxiety of something. Dogs may become phobic of specific objects, animals, or situations.

Phobias can be very difficult to treat, and in some cases may require the help of a behaviourist. It is important to address a phobia as soon as possible, as it can lead to other behavioural problems.

If your dog has a phobia, you will need to work with him to help him overcome it.

## *Low Self-esteem*

Dogs can develop low self-esteem for a variety of reasons. Some dogs may be shy and withdrawn because they were not socialized enough as puppies. Other dogs may become insecure and anxious because they were harshly corrected or scolded by their owners. Dogs may also become low-spirited if they are not given enough exercise or mental stimulation.

Low self-esteem can be difficult to change, but it is important to try. Dogs with low self-esteem may benefit from behaviour modification exercises, such as confidence-building games. It is also important to provide your dog with plenty of socialization, a behaviourist can help you in setting up activities with your dog after analyzing the issue. Never scold or punish your dog for being shy or anxious, as this will only make the problem worse. Instead, try to be understanding and be patient. Help your dog build his confidence by taking things slowly and rewarding him for small accomplishments. Remember, it takes time to change low self-esteem, but it is possible with patience and the right guidance.

If you think your dog may have low self-esteem, please consult with a behaviourist or trainer who can help you assess the problem and come up with a plan to address it.

25

# CHAPTER V

# Calm Confident Companion Skills

This chapter is NOT about how to train your dog — yet the "Calm Confident Companion Skills" I'm going to share with you will help you get exceptional results from the puppy.

This chapter is NOT about teaching your puppy different tricks — yet these skills will prove to be very beneficial in everyday life.

If you are a first-time puppy parent and struggling in finding a good trainer, In my experience, after working with hundreds of dogs and humans, I've found that it is best if you can give training to your puppy, it strengthens the bond between you and the puppy more than you think.

So, what training should you practice with your puppy and why should you practice?

THAT is what this chapter is about.

This chapter will give you 5 skills you need to help your puppy learn which will improve your quality of life with your puppy.

You will learn about obedience fundamentals, you will learn the importance of teaching your puppy to be calm during car rides or how to be in a relaxed state when you take him to a pet-friendly restaurant, and you will also learn to work on his touch and collar sensitivity.

When you implement each of these skills, you will transform the life of your puppy and yours as well, a different dimension of companionship will open for you to enjoy.

These are the five skills that can help any puppy learn to Be Calm, Confident & Obedient in most situations:

1. Obedience Fundamentals
2. Calm Car Rides
3. Relaxing Restaurant Outings
4. Touch Sensitivity
5. Collar Sensitivity

I am going to discuss every skill as a separate section so that we can go deep and you can realize the importance of these 5 skills.

Are you ready?

Let's Begin...

## Obedience Fundamentals

This is the foundation of obedience in your dog and it must be performed daily for 15-20 minutes.

Obedience fundamentals consist of variations of four commands:

1. Sit
2. Stay
3. Down
4. Come

You should start training your dog with these four fundamental commands, you should allocate time and be disciplined about the training.

There should be no distraction during the training session and you should give the session utmost respect if you want your dog to learn discipline and respect.

Most trainers use a lot of excitement because they can't create enough motivation through food, and the reason behind this is that humans keep on feeding amazing delicious tasty treats to dogs daily multiple times.

Your dog or puppy shouldn't have a treat without working for it. They become highly unmotivated in life and start to find other stimulation in their environment and most of the time they become destructive in nature.

So, if you are giving him treats daily, please stop it, so that you don't have to use excitement while training your puppy.

Now, what is wrong with excitement?

Most people think that excitement is happiness but excitement and happiness are two different emotions. When you give a reward to your puppy you are nurturing the state of mind the puppy is in if you want a calm puppy then always give a reward when the puppy is calm.

There are four stages you and your puppy need to clear to become an obedience fundamental champion.

Stages:

1. Performing when the command is given verbally with treats as motivation.
2. Performing when the command is given verbally without treats.
3. Performing when the command is given with hand gestures only.
4. Performing outside the house at a safe place in all the above three stages.

There is no hurry and you should practice all the stages at your own and your puppy's pace, but just make sure that you practice it every day for 15-20 minutes.

Obedience fundamental commands are going to help you control your dog in a lot of different situations like:

- If any of your guests are afraid of dogs, then you can ask your dog to sit and stay.
- You are walking with him and stop to greet your friend, then you can ask your dog to sit beside you with just your hand gestures.
- You can take him to your friend's place and expect him to behave and whenever he starts to get excited, you can calm him down using your hand gestures, no need to shout or yell.
- You can take him to any restaurant and ask him to chill using the down command.
- If you are walking with your dog and want to buy something from a shop, you can ask your dog to stay outside the shop by keeping an eye on him as well initially.

There are a lot of applications of these four commands that's why your and your puppy's mastery over these is essential to have an amazing life.

So, Practice daily and practice with calmness and patience.

## Calm Car Rides

Start taking your puppy on small rides and be calm from the beginning, take him to the car but don't open the gate until he is calm, you can use the obedience fundamentals command to ask him to sit, and then you can open the gate, even if you have opened the gate, the dog should not jump in right away, he should wait for you give the command to enter which you can do by guiding him using the leash.

If the puppy or dog is pacing around then you should leash him to cut down the option to move, the more he moves, the more anxious he will become.

When you do every step with calmness, the dog makes an association of calmness with the car and he starts practising calmness during the journey.

Do this religiously if you want hassle-free car rides with your dog, this skill is definitely going to improve the quality of life of your dog and you.

If your dog is not ok with car rides, you will hesitate to take him to different places but if your dog is ok with car rides then the life of the dog will become limitless.

## Relaxing Restaurant Outings

There are lots of restaurants opening up nowadays that are dog friendly, and to enjoy that, our dog should also be restaurant friendly.

Restaurants provide lots of stimulation to all three senses:

1.  Nose(Yummy Food)
2.  Eyes(People Moving)
3.  Ears(Lots of Sound)

All the stimulation can be overwhelming for a puppy or a dog, so you should start taking your puppy from a training point of view.

After seeing your puppy, lots of people will come running towards him to touch him which will make him more excited, you need to learn to say no to them and ask them to give distance politely because your puppy is under training.

No matter what, do not let them touch the puppy with excitement, you can't expect your puppy to respect the place if the place is not ready to respect the puppy's intimate space.

Do not feed the puppy in the restaurant otherwise, it will be very hard for him to control himself because of so many different scents of different food, he should understand that no matter what he can't get food here.

You don't want your puppy to beg, which he will do if you start feeding him there and with every instance, begging will increase.

He will start nudging you and then he will start barking.

You also have to understand that there is a difference between a well-behaved dog and a well-trained dog.

If you want your puppy to become a well-behaved dog then you must control your urge to feed him when he shows his puppy eyes, control your emotions if you want your dog to learn to be calm even if there are so many activities going on.

Your puppy should not sit on a table or on a chair, because his size will change exponentially as he starts growing up, and then it will become difficult to stop him from climbing on the table or chair because of the habit we helped him develop, he should practice "Down(Obedience Fundamental)" on the floor.

You are going to practice obedience fundamentals here as well, that's why mastery over fundamentals is necessary to have a puppy who succeeds in every situation.

Keep taking the puppy to different restaurants and keep on teaching calmness by remaining calm and confident. Soon, you will have a puppy who will understand what is expected from him whenever his humans take him to any such place.

## *Touch Sensitivity*

Lots of puppies develop Touch Sensitivity while growing up.

Touch sensitivity means they start reacting whenever humans touch a certain part of the puppy's body.

Once your dog develops this, then you are going to have a very hard time with him, he will start snapping, yelping, and doing whatever to protest against being touched.

Taking him to a vet will become a nightmare and You will think 100 times before giving affection to him which will degrade the quality of life of the puppy and the human as well.

So, How to prevent this?

It is very easy, and let me give you the secret to prevent your puppy from developing this kind of damaging sensitivity.

Every day give your puppy a massage, and during that make sure that the puppy is calm and not reacting to your touches.

If he reacts by grabbing your hand by his mouth then just be calm and say no. Make sure that you don't shout or get fearful of his reaction.

Your calmness, quietness, and confidence is the main ingredient of this training, Make sure that you touch every part of his body with calm, confidence, and compassion.

Your puppy will get habitual and make an association of calmness with the human touch.

This training goes a long way because I get many cases in which dogs snap whenever humans try to touch feed or certain parts of the body just because humans failed to build trust between them and the puppy.

Give time in creating trust with your puppy who is going to live with you for 10-15 years.

## *Collar Sensitivity*

Recently I got bitten by a dog who was collar sensitive, and don't get me wrong but any dog can become collar sensitive.

Collar sensitivity is just like touch sensitivity but in this case, a dog reacts whenever someone holds his collar.

He developed this habit of snapping and biting on the hand which is trying to hold the collar because of the way humans behaved when he did the same for the first time.

When you hold the collar of your puppy, and you let him go if he protests then the puppy learns that he can get away from the hold whenever he protests.

Do not let him go!

Every instance of letting him go on his protest whenever you hold his collar is going to increase the intensity of his protest.

He will pull, use his paw, bark, yelp, or try to grab your hand as well. If he is a puppy then don't let him go whenever he is in this protest state.

Only allow him to go when he is calm.

Practice this daily with your puppy, hold his collar, ask him to sit with you, and let him go after a period of time when he is calm.

This way you are going to teach him that calmness helps him to earn freedom.

This is a simple exercise with lots of applications.

You can calm him down by holding his collar whenever he gets into a state which is not expected.

# CHAPTER VI

# Next Step – Join Help Centre

We have reached the last chapter of this guide, and I thank you for taking initiative in learning about dogs and their way of life.

I never had any plans to start something like OhMyDog in my wildest dream. But life is surprising, one step led to another, and somehow OhMyDog came into existence and became what it is now.

I started learning and teaching in 2016 and started loving the idea of helping people understand dog psychology. Since then I have helped countless dogs and humans. I got so much into learning and teaching dog psychology that I left everything else(My IT career)

But as my love for dogs kept on growing, my love for coding(my first love) start coming back as well. I used my IT and teaching skills and created ohmydog website to help people learn more and more from my videos and blog which gave me a chance to restart my IT career as well.

So thank you all for helping me go on this amazing adventure of becoming a self-taught dog behaviourist.

Now, I help dog parents with my experience, and I encourage you to join our help centre (WhatsApp community) so that you can ask your doubts and I try my best to give practical solutions.

So what are you waiting for? Goto ohmydog.rocks to join the help centre and let's connect ♥

# Conclusion

Thank you for reading this guide on how to raise a well-behaved, balanced dog. We hope you have found it helpful and informative. Dogs can be wonderful companions, but they require a lot of care and attention. By understanding their psychology and providing them with the right rituals, you can help your dog live a happy, confident life. If you have any questions or would like to learn more about dog behaviour, please join our help centre.